The Chernobyl Disaster: The History and Legacy of the World's Worst Nuclear Meltdown

By Charles River Editors

A picture of the damage at Chernobyl after the accident

About Charles River Editors

Charles River Editors provides superior editing and original writing services across the digital publishing industry, with the expertise to create digital content for publishers across a vast range of subject matter. In addition to providing original digital content for third party publishers, we also republish civilization's greatest literary works, bringing them to new generations of readers via ebooks.

Sign up here to receive updates about free books as we publish them, and visit Our Kindle Author Page to browse today's free promotions and our most recently published Kindle titles.

Introduction

Tiia Monto's picture of a memorial and the "Chernobyl Nuclear Power Plant sarcophagus," designed to contain the Unit 4 reactor at Chernobyl after the accident

Chernobyl (April 26, 1986)

"The risk projections suggest that by now Chernobyl may have caused about 1000 cases of thyroid cancer and 4000 cases of other cancers in Europe, representing about 0.01% of all incident cancers since the accident. Models predict that by 2065 about 16,000 cases of thyroid cancer and 25,000 cases of other cancers may be expected due to radiation from the accident, whereas several hundred million cancer cases are expected from other causes." – Findings in an article published in the *International Journal of Cancer* in 2006

Uranium is best known for the destructive power of the atom bombs, which ushered in the nuclear era at the end of World War II, but given the effectiveness of nuclear power, nuclear power plants were constructed around the developed world during the second half of the 20th century. While nuclear power plants were previously not an option and thus opened the door to new, more efficient, and more affordable forms of energy for domestic consumption, the use of nuclear energy understandably unnerved people living during the Cold War and amidst ongoing nuclear detonations. After all, the damage wrought on Hiroshima and Nagasaki made clear to everyone what nuclear energy was capable of inflicting, and the health problems encountered by people exposed to the radiation also demonstrated the horrific side effects that could come with the use of nuclear weapons or the inability to harness the technology properly.

The first major accident at a nuclear power plant took place at Three Mile Island in Pennsylvania in 1979, which took nearly 15 years and $1 billion to fully clean up after that disaster, but Three Mile Island paled in comparison to Chernobyl, which to this day remains the most notorious nuclear accident in history. Located in the Ukraine, the Chernobyl power plant was undergoing experiments in the early morning hours of April 26, 1986 when it suffered a series of explosions in one of its nuclear reactors, killing over 30 people at the plant and spread radioactive fallout across a wide swath of the Soviet Union. Although the Soviets would try to cover up just how disastrous the accident at Chernobyl was, it was impossible to hide the full extent of the damage given that radioactive material was affecting Western Europe as well. All told, the accident caused an estimated $18 billion in damages, forced the evacuation of everybody nearby, and continues to produce adverse health effects that are still being felt in the region.

As with Three Mile Island before it, Chernobyl emphatically demonstrated the dangers of nuclear power plants, and it brought about new regulations across the world in an effort to make the use of nuclear energy safer. Meanwhile, scientists and scholars are still studying the effects of the radiation on people exposed to it and continue to come up with estimates of just how deadly Chernobyl will wind up being.

The Chernobyl Disaster chronicles the worst nuclear accident in history and the aftermath of the accident. Along with pictures and a bibliography, you will learn about Chernobyl like never before, in no time at all.

The Chernobyl Disaster: The History and Legacy of the World's Worst Nuclear Meltdown
About Charles River Editors
Introduction
- Chapter 1: Rapid and Precise
- Chapter 2: Explosions
- Chapter 3: The Pressure of the Unseen Rays
- Chapter 4: The Fire Continued to Howl and to Howl
- Chapter 5: Do Not Cause a Panic
- Chapter 6: Come On, Come On
- Chapter 7: They Needed Bags, Shovels, Sand and People
- Chapter 8: The Dozens of Those Who Died
- Chapter 9: The Ash Fell on Pripyat
- Bibliography

Chapter 1: Rapid and Precise

A modern view of the Chernobyl plant from Pripyat, Ukraine

Picture of the reactor hall in Unit 1 at Chernobyl

"What did Akimov and Toptunov, the operators of the nuclear process, feel at the moment when the control rods became stuck along the way and the first terrible shocks were heard from the central hall? It is difficult to say, because both operators died a painful death from radiation without leaving any testimony on this point. But one can imagine what they felt. I am familiar with the feeling operators experience in the first moment of an accident. I have been in their shoes repeatedly when I worked in operation of nuclear power plants. In the first instant, you go numb, an avalanche comes crushing down on your chest, you experience a cold wave of involuntary fear above all at being caught unawares and at first not knowing what to do when the pointers of the recorders and indicating instruments fly in different directions, and your eyes try to follow them all at once when the cause and pattern of the emergency state are still not clear, when at the same time (again involuntarily) you are thinking somewhere deep down, at the third level, about responsibility and the consequences of what has happened. But in the very next instant there comes an unusual clarity of mind and cool headedness. As a consequence, your actions to localize the accident are rapid and precise…" - Grigoriy Medvedev, deputy chief engineer in Unit 1 at the Chernobyl plant and author of *The Truth About Chernobyl*.

On Friday afternoon, April 25, 1986, Grigoriy Medvedev was in a plane flying near what would soon be the site of the worst nuclear disaster in history, which compelled him to describe the before and after. He later wrote, "We flew over the Ukraine, which was buried in its flowering gardens. Some 7 or 8 hours would pass, and a new era would begin for that region, an era of misery and nuclear contamination. Meanwhile, I was looking down at the ground through the window. Kharkov floated by below in a bluish haze. ... The splendid Pripyat River! Its water is brown, apparently because it flows out of the Polesian peat bogs, the current is strong and fast; when you swim, it tried to carry you away."

Indeed, the people living in that region had no reason to think anything would be different as they slept through the early morning hours of Saturday, April 26, 1986. Those who weren't asleep in the industrial city of Chernobyl were mostly working the night shift at the local nuclear power plant, and many of those who arrived at the plant the night before knew that there would be a systems test held sometime that day. This was a standard procedure, and no one gave it much thought when Aleksandr Akimov, the unit chief of that shift, planned to start the test after midnight. His wife, Lyubov, later said, "My husband was a very amiable and sociable person. He had an easy way with people, but without familiarity. An obliging man who found a joy in life. Active in civic work. He was a member of the Pripyat Gorkom. He loved his sons very much. He was thoughtful. He loved to hunt, especially after he went to work in the unit and we bought a car."

Akimov

Even before the test began, something went terribly wrong when a sudden power surge occurred in the number four reactor. The power than dropped from a surge of 1500 MWt to a mere 30, leading Akimov to suggest that the test be cancelled. Nonetheless, Anatoly Dyatlov, the deputy chief engineer supervising the experiment, insisted that they proceed. According to Viktor Grigoryevich Smagin, the shift chief at Unit 4, "Dyatlov was a difficult man to get along with, someone who operated by delayed action. He was accustomed to tell his subordinates: I do not punish at once. I think over what a subordinate has done for at least a day, and when there is no longer any feeling of resentment in my heart, I make a decision....' He had assembled a handful of physicist supervisors from the Far East, where he had worked as chief of a physics laboratory. Orlov and [Anatoliy Andreyevich] Sitnikov, (both killed) also came from there. And many others were friends and comrades from where he had worked before. The general tendency at the Chernobyl plant before the explosion was to thrash the operating personnel on the shifts, and to spare and give incentives to the daytime (non-operating) personnel of the shops. There were usually more emergencies in the turbine hall, fewer in the reactor department. That accounts for the less alert attitude toward the reactor. The feeling was that it was reliable and safe..."

Dyatlov

Chapter 2: Explosions

"Once the lower water lines, through which coolant was fed to the core, had been torn away, the nuclear reactor was altogether without water. Unfortunately, as we realized later, the operators did not understand this or did not wish to believe it, which resulted in an entire chain of wrong moves, over-irradiation, and death which could have been avoided. So—explosions...." - Grigoriy Medvedev

A few minutes after the initial surge, the power level stabilized at 200 MWt and all seemed to be well, but nobody realized at the time that xenon was leaking into the nuclear core, poisoning and destabilizing it. When Akimov began the test around 1:30 a.m., the main water pumps became filled with bubbles caused by the inlet water, which had begun to boil. The power produced by the reactor rose to dangerous levels as the water around the core vaporized and fell from the standard 25 feet in depth to around 8 feet deep. Medvedev later noted, "It was stated at many press conferences that immediately before the explosion the reactor had been reliably shut down, the rods had been inserted in the core. But, as we have already said, the effectiveness of the emergency safety was for all practical purposes nullified because of the flagrant violations of the operating rules. After the AZ button was pressed, the control rods, as has already been stated, entered only about 2.5 meters into the core instead of the assumed 7, and they did not smother the reaction, but on the contrary assisted the prompt-neutron excursion. Nothing was said at a single press conference about this most flagrant mistake of the system's designers, which ultimately served as the main cause of the nuclear disaster."

Still hoping to avert disaster, Akimov disconnected the clutches holding the control rods in the air, hoping that their own weight would then lower them deeper into the water, but they were apparently stuck in place. Soon after that, the control rods seized up and the reactor exploded, hurtling objects around the vicinity, sending dust into the air around the building, and knocking the power out.

Within moments, the room was filled with men reporting that the reactor top had collapsed in on itself and that there was a fire in the turbine hall. Akimov reported the fires and contacted the electrical department, pleading for enough power to control the disaster, but then the phone lines went down. However, Dyatlov refused to believe that the reactor itself had exploded, so he ordered it cooled with a flood of cold water, and even when he learned that the damage was more extensive than he originally thought, he disconnected power to the control rods, still insisting that the reactor was undamaged. As a result, Akimov ordered men to the turbine hall to manually open the cooling system valves, subsequently exposing them to substantial amounts of radiation.

Meanwhile, people throughout the power plant couldn't help but hear the explosions and immediately start to wonder about what was happening. According to one man, "At the time of the explosion, I was right by the dispatcher station, where I was on duty. A powerful discharge of steam was suddenly heard. We paid no importance to it, since discharges of steam had occurred repeatedly while I had worked there. I intended to go off to rest, and at that point there was the explosion. I dashed to the window, after the explosion there were others that followed instantaneously...I saw a black fireball which soared over the roof of the turbine section of Unit 4...In the central hall, it looked like a glow or luminescence. But there was nothing there to burn, only the snout of the reactor. We decided that that glow came from the reactor..."

An aerial photo of the damage done by the explosions

Nikolai Gorbachenko was in the duty room when he heard a loud thud. Though startled, he was not concerned since he assumed it was caused by the turbine in Unit 4 being shut down for testing. However, when he heard a second thud, he became concerned, especially once the lights in the building went out. He picked up the phone only to find it, too, was not working. Looking out his door, he noticed that the hallway was full of steam and dust, while the needles on the radiation counters flipped back and forth like a waving flag. He later described the scene: "At the moment of the explosion and afterward, I was at the dosimetry panel. There were several shudders with terrible force. I thought: everything, the roof. But I saw that I was alive, I was standing on my feet. Another comrade, my assistant Pshenichnikov, quite a young lad, was there with me at the dosimetry panel. I opened the door to the corridor of the deaerator galleries, clouds of white dust and steam were coming from there. There was the characteristic smell of steam. There were still flashes of discharges. Short circuits. The panels of Unit 4 were immediately extinguished on the dosimetry panel. No readings. I did not know what was happening in the unit, what the radiation situation was. The emergency signal system was working on the panels of Unit 3 (we had a single panel for the entire stage of construction). All the instruments had gone off scale. I pushed the toggle switch for the unit control room, but the switchboard had no power."

Of course, everyone at the plant knew the biggest danger in the event of some sort of accident, as Gorbachenko noted: "I tried to determine the radiation situation in the room where I was and in the corridor outside the door. I had only the DRGZ radiometer rated for 1,000 microroentgens per second. It went off scale. I had another instrument with a scale that went up to 1,000 roentgens, but when I turned it on, as luck would have it, it burned out. There were no others. Then, I went over to the unit control room and reported the situation to Akimov. Everywhere it was off scale at 1,000 microroentgens per second. Probably about 4 roentgens per hour. If that was so, then we could work about 5 hours. Depending, of course, on the conditions of the emergency situation. Akimov said I should go around the unit and determine the dosimetric situation. I went up to the level +27 through the staircase-elevator well, but I went no further. The instrument was off scale everywhere. Petya Palamarchuk came, and he and I went to Room 604 to look for Volodya Shashenok... "

Gorbachenko and Palamarchuk found Shashenok unconscious in the instrument room, trapped under a large beam and covered with severe burns caused by exposure to both steam and radiation. They carried him out of the building and ordered him transported to the nearest hospital, where he died a few hours later.

Meanwhile, unaware that Shashenok's hand had left a radioactive burn on his own back, Gorbachenko began looking for Valery Knodemchuk, who was supposed to be operating the main circulating pump that night. Gorbachenko could not find him, and it was later determined that Knodemchuk had died instantly after being crushed by the debris or being vaporized in the wake of the explosions. Whatever the reason, his body was never found.

Oleg Genrikh and Anatoly Kurguz were in a control room when the explosion occurred, and it was loud enough to blow out their observation window and put the lights out. Both were burned by escaping steam, Kurguz more severely, and they joined two other men in escaping the building. When they passed Dyatlov in the hall, he ordered them to take decontamination showers and then to report to the plant infirmary. Later, Kurguz went by ambulance to the hospital.

Reactor section foreman Valeriy Ivanovich Perevozchenko had seen the huge blocks that sat on top of the Upper Biological Shield begin to bounce around as the building began to shake. He ran down the staircase to the control room to warn his coworkers, but by the time he arrived, the reactor had exploded. As his skin turned brown right before his eyes, he tried to locate the men he knew had been working nearest the explosion. However, he soon had to give up, overcome by nausea and weakness.

Alexander Yuvchenko was in his office when the explosions occurred, and he later recalled, "There was a heavy thud. A couple of seconds later, I felt a wave come through the room. The thick concrete walls were bent like rubber. I thought war had broken out. We started to look for Knodemchuk...but he had been by the pumps and had been vaporized. Steam wrapped around everything; it was dark and there was a horrible hissing noise. There was no ceiling, only sky; a sky full of stars. I remember thinking how beautiful it was."

Though he was badly burned himself, he moved quickly through the building looking for his co-workers. He then joined three other men who had been sent to lower the radioactive control rods to safety. A physically imposing man, Yuvchenko opened and held open the huge door to the damaged room while the others went inside to do their work. Though the three were in the room for less than a minute, they all received a lethal dose of radiation and were dead within two weeks. For his part, Yuvchenko reported that though he too had received radiation burns on his shoulder and legs, "You don't feel anything at the time. We had no idea there was so much radiation. We met a guy with a doseometer and the needle was just off the dial. But even then, we were still only thinking 'Rats, this means the end of our careers in the nuclear industry.' We all thought, 'We've been exposed now, this has happened on our watch' and set about doing what we could. After about an hour, I started to vomit uncontrollably. My throat was very sore. We were thinking we might have had 20, perhaps 50rem. But there was a man there who'd been involved in a nuclear accident in the submarine fleet, he said it was more serious than that. 'You don't vomit at 50,' he said."

After collapsing at around 6:00 a.m., Yuvchenko was taken to the hospital, where he would remain for the next year.

Chapter 3: The Pressure of the Unseen Rays

A picture of nuclear fuel leaking out into the basement of the power plant

"[Valeriy Ivanovich] Perevozchenko...rushed into the corridor...intending to look for his subordinates who could have been in the rubble. The very first thing he did was to run to the broken windows and look out. There was an extremely strong smell freshness, like the air after a thunderstorm, but many times stronger. It was nighttime in the yard outside. Red reflections from the burning roof of the turbine hall in the low nighttime sky. When there was no wind, the air usually had no smell. But at this point, Perevozchenko felt as it were the pressure of the unseen rays that were running all through him. He was seized by some inner panic fear coming from the death of his organism. But his anxiety for his comrades was uppermost. He stuck his head quite far out and looked to the right. He realized that the reactor unit was destroyed. Where the walls of the main circulating pump room had been, he saw in the darkness a heap of broken structural elements, pipe, and equipment. Up above...He raised his head. The spaces of the drum separators were not there either. That meant an explosion in the central hall. ... There was a fire burning his lungs. That first oppressiveness passed, Perevozchenko felt an inner heat in his chest, in his face, throughout his entire being. As though he had completely burned up from within." - Grigoriy Medvedev

In the minutes after the explosion, Dyatlov was frequently informed of the damage to the plant, but he continued to insist that it was not caused by the reactor exploding but by an explosion in the emergency tank. In fact, he reported a "tank explosion" to his supervisor, V.P. Bryukhanov, when Bryukhanov arrived at the plant less than an hour later. Meanwhile, Dyatlov ordered Reactor 3 shut down and told Akimov to call in the day shift to help with the crisis. Dyatlov then met up with Gorbachenko, and the two began to move around the outside of the plant, trying to ascertain how much damage had been done. By the time they returned to the duty room, both men very physically ill and had begun to vomit. They were then transported to a nearby hospital for treatment.

After Dyatlov was sent to the hospital, Chief Engineer N.M. Fomin took charge of the situation, and he initially kept ordering water to be poured into what he had been told was an intact reactor. However, when he had to constantly replace the staff forcing water into the area as they became overwhelmed with radiation sickness, he ordered Anatoliy Sitnikov, then the deputy chief engineer for operation, to climb to the top of the roof and give him a visual evaluation of the reactor. Sitnikov reported back to Fomin at 10:00 AM and informed him that the reactor was indeed destroyed. Though this information cost the man his life, Fomin still refused to believe him and kept water flowing in the crumbling reactor. All this accomplished was to spread the radioactive material through broken pipes and throughout the other buildings at the site.

By this time, those inside the plant had been in touch with others higher up the chain of command and had informed them of the accident, but in many cases, they were inadvertently misinforming them. Alfa Fedorovna Martynova mentioned one call she and her husband received that fateful night: "On 26 April 1986 at 0300 hours, the intercity phone rang in our house. Bryukhanov was calling [V.V.] Maryin from Chernobyl. When he finished the conversation, Maryin told me: 'A horrible accident at Chernobyl; but the reactor is intact...' He quickly dressed and called for his car. Just before he left, he called the highest leadership of the party's Central Committee up through channels. First of all, Frolyshev. He in turn called Dolgikh. Dolgikh called Gorbachev and the members of the Politburo. After that, he left for the Central Committee. At 0800 hours, he called home and asked me to prepare his things for a trip."

Even as those on the ground in Unit 4 were trying to remedy the situation, no matter how well or ill informed they were, some people working in different units around the nuclear plant braced for the worst and decided to take no chances. Yuriy Bagdasarov was a shift chief in Unit 3 at the time the explosion occurred, and to his credit, he immediately assumed the worst and saved his own life, as well that of his subordinates, by ordering everyone into protective gear at the first sign of danger. After trying and failing to get permission from Fomin to shut down the power to his reactor, he shut it down anyway, preventing further spread of the contaminated water flowing from the damaged reactor in Unit 4. Thus, he likely prevented yet another disaster from occurring in the form of a meltdown of the number 3 reactor.

Chapter 4: The Fire Continued to Howl and to Howl

"Akimov and Toptunov had already run up several times to the reactor to see the effect of the flow of water from the second emergency feedwater pump. But the fire continued to howl and to howl. Akimov and Toptunov were already reddish brown from the nuclear sunburn, already nausea had upset their insides, Dyatlov, Davetbayev, and people from the turbine hall were already at the medical unit, they had already sent unit shift chief Vladimir Alekseyevich Babichev to replace Akimov, but…Akimov and Toptunov were not leaving. One can only bow his head in the face of their bravery and fearlessness. After all, they condemned themselves to a certain death. Nevertheless, all of their actions followed from a false original premise: the reactor was intact! They were utterly unable to believe that the reactor had been destroyed, that the water was not going to it, but, taking the nuclear trash along with it, it was flowing to the minus levels, soaking the cableways and high-voltage distribution equipment and creating a threat of taking power from all three power-generating units that were operating." - Grigoriy Medvedev

Within minutes of the experiment going wrong, the necessary alerts had gone out, and firefighters arrived within minutes to fight the fires produced by the exploded reactor. However, given that some of the employees didn't understand the full extent of the fallout, including the man nominally in charge, the firefighters entered the situation without the kind of attire that could properly protect them from radiation, and while many of them knew what kind of dangers they were in, others did not. Grigorii Khmel drove one of the first trucks to Chernobyl that morning and later claimed, "We arrived there at 10 or 15 minutes to two in the morning...We saw graphite scattered about. Misha asked: 'Is that graphite?' I kicked it away. But one of the fighters on the other truck picked it up. 'It's hot,' he said. The pieces of graphite were of different sizes, some big, some small, enough to pick them up...We didn't know much about radiation. Even those who worked there had no idea. There was no water left in the trucks. Misha filled a cistern and we aimed the water at the top. Then those boys who died went up to the roof – Vashchik, Kolya and others, and Volodya Pravik...They went up the ladder ... and I never saw them again."

A picture of pieces of a graphite moderator from the core of the exploded reactor

On the other hand, some firefighters remembered that they were aware of the radiation risks, including Anatoli Zakharov, who asserted, "I remember joking to the others, 'There must be an incredible amount of radiation here. We'll be lucky if we're all still alive in the morning.'...Of course we knew! If we'd followed regulations, we would never have gone near the reactor. But it was a moral obligation – our duty. We were like kamikaze."

All the same, their training dominated their thinking and took over, leading them again and again to put themselves in harm's way to fight the fire raging through the plant. They were where the fire was, even into the very heart of the reactor chamber, and some gave their lives without even knowing that's what they were doing. V. V. Bulava, who drove one of the first trucks to the Chernobyl plant that day, remembered, "I received an order to put myself under the disposition of Lieutenant Khmel. I went there. I set up the truck where the water was and turned on the water supply. My truck had just been repaired, it was just like new, it smelled of fresh paint. The wheels also had new tires and tubes. Just as I was approaching the unit, I heard something strike the right front fender. I jumped out to see what it was. There it was—a piece of reinforcement steel had pierced the tire, it was sticking out of the wheel and catching the fender...It had just been repaired, such a pity. But for the present I hooked the machine up to the water, there was no time. And then I turned on the pumps, sat in the cab, but that piece of iron kept pestering me. I got out and saw that it had punctured the tube and was celebrating. No, I thought, I will not put up with anything like that. I climbed down from the truck and pulled at the damned thing. It did not give. It gave me plenty of trouble...And ultimately I ended up in the

Moscow clinic with deep radiation burns on my hands. Had I known, I would have put on gloves. That's life..."

Thus, even as they were being exposed to potentially lethal doses of radiation, the firefighters continued to try to prevent the spread of the blaze to other reactors within the plant. In the end, however, the fire would continue to burn in Unit 4 two full weeks, until it was extinguished on May 10 with the use of liquid nitrogen and the efforts of helicopters dropping materials on it from above.

In this picture, Major Leonid Telyatnikov, the Commander of the Chernobyl Fire Brigade, is being awarded a prize for his actions. Telyatnikov survived acute radiation sickness in the wake of Chernobyl but later died of cancer in his 50s.

Chapter 5: Do Not Cause a Panic

"More than 100 people had already been sent to the medical unit. It was time to be reasonable. But no—the folly of Bryukhanov and Fomin continued: 'The reactor is intact! Pour water into the reactor!' But in the depths of his soul Bryukhanov apparently had still taken note of the information from Sitnikov and Solovyev [this name has been changed] and he requested Moscow's 'go-ahead' to evacuate Pripyat. But a clear order came from Shcherbina, with whom his consultant L. P. Drach was in telephone contact…Do not cause a panic. And at that time Pripyat, a city of nuclear power plant workers, was waking up. Almost all the children had set off for school...." - Grigoriy Medvedev

As a crisis of unknown proportions was taking place at the Chernobyl plant during the early hours of April 26, nearby residents (many of whom worked at the plant during different shifts, were starting to wake up), and their first thoughts that morning were quite different depending on where they lived. 8:00 a.m. was the designated time for each day's shift change at Chernobyl, but of course, the 26th would not be a day like any other, as plant worker Viktor Grigoryevich Smagin explained, "I was supposed to replace Aleksandr Akimov at 0800 hours on the morning of 26 April 1986. I had a good sleep that night. I heard no explosions. I woke at 0700 hours and went out on the balcony to have a smoke. From my apartment on the 14th floor I have a good view of the nuclear power plant. I looked in that direction and immediately realized that the central hall of my own Unit 4 had been destroyed. There was fire and smoke over the unit. I realized that things were rotten. I rushed to the telephone to call the unit control room, but the phones had already been cut off. To keep the information from leaking. I got ready to leave. I told my wife to close the doors and windows tightly. Not to let the children out of the house. Not to go out herself either. To sit at home until I came back...I ran out into the street to the bus stop. But the bus did not go up to the plant. Soon, they sent a radio message saying that they would not go to the second passageway as usual, but to Unit 1. Everything there had already been cut off by the police. The officers were not letting anyone through. Then, I showed my 24-hour pass for supervisory operating personnel, and they let me through, but reluctantly. ... I changed clothes quickly, not knowing at that point that I would be coming back from the unit to the medical station with severe nuclear sunburn and a dose of 280 rads."

On the other hand, Lyudmila Aleksandlrovna Kharitonova, a senior engineer at the Chernobyl Nuclear Power Plant, remembered the beginning of that morning differently: "On Saturday, 26 April 1986, all preparations had been made for the May Day holiday. The weather was warm that day. It was springtime. The gardens were in flower. My husband, chief of the section for adjustment of the ventilation, intended to go off with the children to the dacha after work. I had been washing since morning and hanging out bed linen on the balcony. Even by evening, millions of particles had accumulated on it. Among most of the construction and installation workers, no one knew anything as yet. Then, something leaked out about the accident and the fire at Unit 4. But what had actually happened no one really knew. The children went to school, small children played in the street in sandboxes, they rode their bicycles. By the evening of 26 April, the radioactivity in the hair and clothing of all of them was already high, but we did not know that at the time. In our street, not far away they were selling tasty doughnuts. It was an ordinary day off."

Even among those who saw the damage from a distance, some figured it was nothing to worry about. Grigoriy Medvedev offered up an account of how life still seemed quite normal to fishermen despite their proximity to the plant: "Fishermen, they seemed to replace one another practically all and all night at the place where the drain entered the cooling pond; everyone fished when he was not on duty. The water was always warm after going through the turbines and heat-exchanging equipment, and there are plenty of bites. Also, it was spring, spawning, and the fishing was just excellent. It is about 2 km from the fishing place to Unit 4. ... When they heard the explosions and saw the fire, many remained there fishing until morning, while others, feeling an incomprehensible anxiety, a sudden dryness in their throat and burning in their eyes, went back to Pripyat. People had become accustomed not to pay attention to noises like the cannon like booms when the safety valves operated, which were like explosions, but the fire.... They would put it out. It's nothing much!"

Of course, those arriving at the plant that morning soon learned that something had gone terribly wrong just a few hours earlier, and while some responded fearfully, many acted heroically. Some, like Viktor Smagin, were simply anxious to see for themselves what was going on, and what they found was chaos, with the stress of the situation creating all kinds of short-tempered arguments. Smagin wrote, "I was in a hurry, I put on the cotton coveralls, the high boots, the cap, the 'respirator-200' and ran along the long corridor of the deaerator galleries (which connected all four units) toward Unit 4. In the room that housed the 'Skala' computer, there had been a break, water was flowing from the ceiling onto the cabinets containing the equipment. At that point, I still did not know that the water was highly radioactive. There was no one in the room. ... I went on further. Krasnozhon, deputy chief of the radiation safety department, was already at work in the room containing the dosimetry panel. ... Samoylenko, chief of the night shift of dosimetrists, was also in the room. ... Samoylenko was pressing the point that the radiation was immense, while Krasnozhon was saying that it was possible to work 5 hours on the assumption of 25 rems. 'How long to work, guys?' I asked, interrupting their squabble. 'The background is 1,000 microroentgens per second, that is, 3.6 roentgens per hour. You can work 5 hours on the assumption of accumulating 25 rems!' 'It's all lies,' Samoylenko summed up. Krasnozhon became enraged all over again."

In addition to the emotionally charged atmosphere that was obviously leading to angry reactions, the radioactively charged atmosphere was demonstrating its own effects, as those who had already been exposed to high doses of radiation were experiencing all kinds of physical reactions, from nausea to panic. Smagin continued, "All the windows in the corridor of the dearator galleries had been broken by the explosion. There was a very acrid smell of ozone. My organism felt the strong radiation. But they say that there are no such sense organs. Evidently, still there is something. There was an unpleasant feeling in the chest—an arbitrary sense of panic, but I controlled myself and kept my grip. It was already light, and the pile of debris was already quite visible through the window. Something black was strewn everywhere on the asphalt. I took a look—so it was reactor graphite! Not bad! I understood that the reactor was in a bad way. But the full reality of what had happened still did not get through to me."

As Smagin's account indicates, hysteria was breaking out at the plant, and panicked administrators struggled to decide what to do next. Vladimir Pavlovich Voloshko, the chairman of Communist Party Committee in Pripyat, was at the plant by then and described the hectic nature of the situation at Chernobyl: "The entire day of 26 April Bryukhanov was beside himself, like a man who was lost. Fomin, he would cry in the pauses between issuing orders, he had lost his self-confidence. Both of them more or less came to themselves by evening, by the time Shcherbina arrived. As though he could have brought salvation with him...They sent Sitnikov, an excellent physicist, to take 1,500 roentgens! And then they didn't listen to him when he reported that the reactor had been destroyed. Out of the 5,500 people on the plant labor force, 4,000 vanished to parts unknown on the very first day... "

In fact, there was no longer anything that could be done to save the destroyed Unit 4, a realization that managers probably should have reached within minutes of the explosions, not several hours after. Regardless, it was time to turn their attention to saving the people in the plant and living around it, people whose lives became more endangered with every minute that information was withheld. Not surprisingly, there was a lockdown that ensured no one from the power plant went home at the end of their shift that day, and this worried workers' families. Lyubov Nikolayevna Akimova, the wife of Unit 4 chief Aleksandr Akimov, recalled, "The entire 1st half of the day I ran around, asked everyone, looked for my husband. Everyone already knew that there had been an accident, and I was seized by still greater anxiety. I went to Voloshko in the gorispolkom, to Gamanyuk in the party gorkom. Finally, after inquiring of many people, I learned that he was at the medical unit. I rushed over there. But they would not let me in. They said he was receiving an intravenous injection at the time. I did not leave, I went up to the window of his ward. Soon he came to the window. His face was reddish brown. When he saw me, he began to laugh, he was overexcited, he reassured me, asked me about the boys through the glass. It seemed to me that at that point he was somehow particularly glad that he had the sons. He said that I should not let them go into the street. He was even cheerful, and I felt a bit reassured." Akimov died two weeks later from the radiation poisoning he received that day.

More and more people in the area around the Chernobyl power plant learned that something was going on there as the hours passed on April 26, but few realized how serious the situation was, and they had no reliable way of knowing either. Nadezhda Petrovna Vygovskaya lived in the nearby town of Pripyat with her husband and son and wrote about that Saturday: "That morning no one suspected anything. I sent my son to school, my husband went to the barber's. I'm preparing lunch when my husband comes back. 'There's some sort of fire at the nuclear plant,' he says. 'They're saying we are not to turn off the radio.' ... I can still see the bright-crimson glow, it was like the reactor was glowing. This wasn't any ordinary fire, it was some sort of shining. It was pretty. I'd never seen anything like it in the movies. That evening everyone spilled out onto their balconies, and those who didn't have them went to friends' houses. We were on the ninth floor, we had a great view. People brought their kids out, picked them up, said, 'Look! Remember!' And these were people who worked at the reactor — engineers, workers, physics instructors. They stood in the black dust, talking, breathing, wondering at it. People came from all around on their cars and their bikes to have a look. We didn't know that death could be so beautiful. Though I wouldn't say that it had no smell — it wasn't a spring or an autumn smell, but something else, and it wasn't the smell of earth. My throat tickled, and tears came to my eyes."

During the 26th, Lyudmila Kharitonova thought that it might be best to get her family away from the area for a while, explaining, "We decided to go to the dacha (a country house), but the police were stationed on the road and would not let us out of town. We went back home. Strange, but we still perceived the accident as something separate from our private life. After all, there had been accidents before, but they concerned only the plant itself...After lunch, they began to wash the streets of the city. But this did not attract attention. It was something ordinary on a hot summer day. The sprinkler trucks were nothing unusual in the summer. An ordinary peaceful situation. Though I did somehow pay passing attention to the white foam in the gutters, but I paid it no importance. I thought that the water pressure was high. A group of neighborhood children were riding their bikes on the overpass; from there, you had a good view of the unit there the accident had occurred from the direction of Yanov Station. We were to learn later that this was the most radioactive place in the city, because the cloud of radioactive discharge had passed there. But that became clear later, while at the time, the morning of 26 April, the children were simply interested in looking at the reactor burning. Those children later developed serious radiation disease."

Ultimately, word began to spread that there had been a serious accident, but the government still gave no order to evacuate. Instead, as Kharitonova remembered, "After lunch, our children came back from school. They had been warned there not to go out in the street, to do a housecleaning with water, that was when people first realized that it was serious. Different people learned about the accident at different times, but by the evening of 26 April almost everyone knew, but still the reaction was calm, since all the stores, schools, and institutions were open. We thought that that meant that it was not so dangerous. It became more disturbing as evening approached. This uneasiness spread from who knows where, perhaps from the soul within, perhaps from the air in which the metallic odor had become strong. What it was, I cannot even say precisely. But metallic... In the evening, the fire was more intense. They said the graphite was burning. People saw the fire from far away, but they paid no particular attention. 'Something is burning...' 'The firemen have put it out....' 'It is still burning.'..."

As those at the plant began planning what to do next, a shift in leadership occurred from those who had scientific knowledge of how the plant worked to those who had the administrative experience needed to organize the next steps. Grigoriy Medvedev detailed just part of the chain of command in his book: "At the beginning of the eighties, the nuclear power industry sector was organized in the Central Committee, Maryin headed it, and then finally he had assistants. G.A. Shasharin, an experienced nuclear engineer who had worked for many years operating nuclear power plants and would in future be deputy minister of power for the operation of nuclear plants, became one of them. It was with him that Maryin was at that point riding to the damaged unit in Kizima's GAZ automobile. On the way, they met buses and private automobiles. The spontaneous evacuation had begun. Some had left Pripyat forever even during the day on 26

April with their families and radioactive belongings, without waiting for the orders of the local authorities."

G.A. Shasharin had trained as an engineer and now brought his structural and organizational expertise to bear on the situation. He later explained,

> "On the way from Kiev to Pripyat, I told [A.I.] Mayorets about the working groups. I had thought about this earlier, during the flight from Simferopol to Kiev. Here is the list of groups which I proposed:
>
> 1) a group to study the causes of the accident and the plant's safety....
>
> 2) a group to study the radiation situation around the nuclear plant....
>
> 3) a group to repair the damage and restore operations....
>
> 4) a group to evaluate the need to evacuate the population of Pripyat and nearby farms and villages....
>
> 5) a group to provide instruments, equipment, and supplies..."

However, even as Shasharin was laying out a strategy for dealing with the crisis, many of those around him were dragging their feet, reluctant to take the lead and thus potentially have to take the responsibility and blame for the decisions that were subsequently made. Vladimir Nikolayevich Shishkin was the deputy chief of Soyuzelektromontazh of USSR Minenergo, and he was present at the discussions about what to do about Pripyat. He reported, "It seemed that all those responsible for the catastrophe wanted one thing—to postpone the moment of full recognition, when all the i's would be dotted. They wanted, as was customarily done before Chernobyl, for responsibility and blame to be spread ever so quietly over everyone. That was the reason for this procrastination when every minute was precious, when delay threatened the city's innocent population with irradiation. When it was already in everyone's mind, the word 'evacuation' was beating against people's skulls...But the reactor was burning all that time. The graphite was burning, spewing millions of curies of radioactivity into the sky. In spite of the problematical and even grave situation at the damaged unit, the situation in Pripyat is businesslike and calm,' Gamanyuk, first secretary of the Pripyat Party Gorkom, reported to Mayorets (at the time of the accident he was in the medical unit for an examination, but on the morning of 26 April he left his hospital bed and went to work). 'No panic or disorder. Normal, ordinary life on a day off. Children are playing in the streets, athletic competitions are taking place, classes in the schools. Even weddings are being celebrated. Today, they have celebrated 16 weddings of Komsomol young people. We put a stop to false rumors and loose talk."

Some of those in charge thought that there would be no need to evacuate anyone if they could just stop the radioactive material from leaving the plant. Shasharin recalled, "Later, we went up in the helicopter with Maryin and the deputy chairman of Gosatomenergonadzor and Sidorenko, corresponding member of the USSR Academy of Sciences. We hovered over the unit at an altitude of 250 to 300 meters. It seems the pilot had a dosimeter. Although no radiometer. At that altitude, the radiation was 300 roentgens per hour. The upper slab had been heated to a bright yellow color by contrast with the bright cherry color reported by Prushinskiy. Which meant that the temperature in the reactor had risen. The slab was not as crooked where it lay on the shaft as l later, when they threw in the bags of sand. The weight slewed it around. At this point, it had finally become clear that the reactor was destroyed. Sidorenko proposed throwing about 40 tons of lead into the reactor in order to reduce the radiation. I was categorically opposed. That kind of weight from an altitude of 200 meters was an immense dynamic load. It would make a hole all the way through, right down to the bubbler pond, and the entire melted core would flow down into the water of the pond. Then you would have to run wherever your legs would take you."

While the ongoing fire had been a source of fascination throughout much of April 26, the fact that it was still burning by nightfall led many ordinary citizens in the vicinity to assume something was seriously wrong. Nadezhda Vygovskaya wrote, "I didn't sleep all night, and I heard the neighbors walking around upstairs, also not sleeping. They were carrying stuff around, banging things, maybe they were packing their belongings. I fought off my headache with Citramon tablets. In the morning I woke up and looked around and I remember feeling — this isn't something I made up later, I thought it right then — something isn't right, something has changed forever. At eight that morning there were already military people on the streets in gas masks. When we saw them on the streets, with all the military vehicles, we didn't grow frightened — on the contrary, it calmed us down. Since the army has come to our aid, everything will be fine. We didn't understand then that the peaceful atom could kill, that man is helpless before the laws of physics. All day on the radio they were telling people to prepare for an evacuation: they'd take us away for three days, wash everything, check it over. The kids were told to take their school books. Still, my husband put our documents and our wedding photos into his briefcase. The only thing I took was a gauze kerchief in case the weather turned bad."

Chapter 6: Come On, Come On

Picture of a radioactivity warning sign in Pripyat

"He had become the first chairman of the government commission to prepare the damage of the nuclear disaster at Chernobyl. Paler than usual, with his lips pressed tightly and the imperious look of the deep folds in his lean cheeks, he was calm, collected, and concentrated. At that point, he still did not realize that around, both on the street and indoors, the air was saturated with radioactivity, was emitting gamma and beta rays, absolutely, indifferent as to who was irradiated—the devil's own, ministers or ordinary mortals. He was endowed with immense power, but he was a human being, and it took the course with him that it takes in a human being: first, the storm would build underneath against the background of external calm, and then, when he had figured something out and was outlining the strategies, the real storm would burst out, a vicious storm of haste and impatience: faster, faster! Come on, come on!" - Grigoriy Medvedev

Finally, the decision to evacuate nearby areas was made. Shcherbina announced to his fellow administrators, "We are evacuating the city on the morning of 27 April. Bring up all 1,100 buses during the night to the highway between Chernobyl and Pripyat. You, General Bedrov, please set up sentries at every house. Let no one in the street. In the morning, civil defense will announce the necessary information to the population over the radio. And also state the exact time of the evacuation. Carry potassium iodide tablets around to people at home. Enlist Komsomol members for that purpose."

With those instructions in place, an excavation order was broadcast to the residents of Pripyat: "For the attention of the residents of Pripyat! The City Council informs you that due to the accident at Chernobyl Power Station in the city of Pripyat the radioactive conditions in the vicinity are deteriorating. The Communist Party, its officials and the armed forces are taking necessary steps to combat this. Nevertheless, with the view to keep people as safe and healthy as possible, the children being top priority, we need to temporarily evacuate the citizens in the nearest towns of Kiev Oblast. For these reasons, starting from April 27, 1986 2 pm each apartment block will be able to have a bus at its disposal, supervised by the police and the city officials. It is highly advisable to take your documents, some vital personal belongings and a certain amount of food, just in case, with you. The senior executives of public and industrial facilities of the city has decided on the list of employees needed to stay in Pripyat to maintain these facilities in a good working order. All the houses will be guarded by the police during the evacuation period. Comrades, leaving your residences temporarily please make sure you have turned off the lights, electrical equipment and water and shut the windows. Please keep calm and orderly in the process of this short-term evacuation."

Thus, that was how the residents of Pripyat suddenly found themselves boarding hundreds of buses to be taken away from their home, perhaps forever, without knowing where they were going. G.N. Petrov was one of those who left that day: "At exactly 1400 hours, the buses came to every entrance. They cautioned us once again over the radio: dress lightly, take a minimum of things, we would be coming back in 3 days. Even then, the involuntary thought flickered: if many things were taken, then even 1,000 buses would not be enough. Most people obeyed and did not even take what money they had. But in general our people are good: they joked, they cheered up each other, they reassured the children. They would say to them: we are going to see grandma...to the film festival...to the circus.... The adults and the children were pale, sad, and silent. Forced cheerfulness and anxiety were in the air together with the radiation. But it was all efficient. Many people had gone downstairs ahead of time and crowded outside with their children. They kept asking them to go back inside the entrance. When they announced the boarding, we went out of the entrance and right into the bus. Those who lingered behind ran from bus to bus, simply taking unnecessary rems. And so, in a day of peaceful, ordinary life, we had taken more than enough both outside and inside."

Alexey Akindinov's "Chernobyl. Last day of Pripyat"

A 2001 picture of an abandoned residence near Pripyat

Thousands left Pripyat that day, all of them in fear, concerned about their own health, their futures and the lives of their other family members. They had a long, hard journey ahead of them, one that would last long past the moment when the literal trip ended. However, plenty of them were up for the task, as Nadezhda Vygovskaya recalled: "As we were leaving Pripyat there was an army column heading back in the other direction. There were so many military vehicles, that's when I grew frightened. But I couldn't shake the feeling that this was all happening to someone else. I was crying, looking for food, sleeping, hugging my son, calming him down, but inside, this constant sense that I was just an observer. In Kiev they gave us some money, but we couldn't buy anything: hundreds of thousands of people had been uprooted and they'd bought everything up and eaten everything. Many had heart attacks and strokes, right there at the train stations, on the buses. I was saved by my mother. She'd lived a long time and had lost everything more than once. ... Now she said, "We have to get through it. After all, we're alive. I remember one thing: we're on the bus, everyone's crying. A man up front is yelling at his wife. "I can't believe you'd be so stupid! Everyone else brought their things, and all we've got are these three-liter bottles!" The wife had decided that since they were taking the bus, she might as well bring some empty pickling bottles for her mother, who was on the way. They had these big bulging sacks next to their seats, we kept tripping over them the whole way to Kiev, and that's what they came to Kiev with."

Of course, one of the problems facing those coordinating the evacuation was the question of where to take the refugees, especially because many of the villages around the area were already crowded with people who had left before the official evacuation went into effect. G.N. Petrov observed, "We drove to Ivankov (60 km from Pripyat) and there were scattered among the villages. Not everyone took us in willingly. One well-off peasant would not let my family into his immense brick house, not because of the dangerous radiation (he did not understand about that, and explanations had no effect on him), but out of greed. He had not built it, he said, to let strangers in.... Many who had left the buses in Ivankov went on further toward Kiev by foot. Some hitched rides. A helicopter pilot I knew told me only later what he had seen from the air: huge crowds of lightly dressed people, women with children, elderly people, going along the road and the shoulders toward Kiev. He had seen them even in the area of Irpen and Brovary. The vehicles were stuck in those crowds, just as they would have been in a cattle drive. You often see something like that in the films in Central Asia, and you immediately think of a comparison, even if a bad one. And the people trudging, trudging, trudging... "

For those not in the vicinity, the state-controlled television station simply broadcast to others around the Soviet Union on April 28, "There has been an accident at the Chernobyl Nuclear Power Plant. One of the nuclear reactors was damaged. The effects of the accident are being remedied. Assistance has been provided for any affected people. An investigative commission has been set up." However, the understated nature of the announcement couldn't fool everyone, and many were afraid to have any type of contact with those who had been exposed to the radiation. Nadezhda Vygovskaya noted, "From the very first I felt that we were Chernobylites, that we were already a separate people. Our bus stopped overnight in a village; people slept on the floor in a school, others in a club. There was nowhere to go. One woman invited us to sleep at her house. 'Come,' she said, 'I'll put down some linen for you. I feel bad for your boy.' Her friend started dragging her away from us. 'Are you crazy? They're contaminated!' When we settled in Mogilev and our son started school, he came back the very first day in tears. They put him next to a girl who said she didn't want to sit with him, he was radioactive. Our son was in the fourth grade, and he was the only one from Chernobyl in the class. The other kids were afraid of him, they called him 'Shiny.' His childhood had ended so early."

Chapter 7: They Needed Bags, Shovels, Sand and People

"Gen Antoshkin gave up his place on the roof of the 'Pripyat' Hotel to Colonel Nesterov so that the latter would guide the light, and he himself would go up in the air. For a long time, he could not figure out where the reactor was. If you were not familiar with the unit's structure, it was difficult to get your bearings. He realized that knowledgeable assembly workers or operation personnel had to be taken on the 'bomb runs'…The reconnoitering was done, the flight approaches to the reactor were determined. They needed bags, shovels, sand, and people who would fill the bags and road them into the helicopters. General Antoshkin expounded all this to Shcherbina. All of them in the party gorkom were coughing, their throats were dry, they had difficulty speaking." - Grigoriy Medvedev

Although the officials in charge had finally ordered an evacuation, the reactor itself was still belching out radiation at an alarming rate, and it still had to be stopped. It was at this time that Major General N.T. Antoshkin stepped in. According to G.A. Shasharin, "Air Force Gen Antoshkin did very good work. A vigorous and businesslike general, he gave no one any peace and pestered them all. At some 500 meters from the gorkom, near the 'Pripyat' Cafe they found a pile of excellent sand near the river terminal. The hydraulic dredges had built it up for construction of the city's new residential areas. They brought bundle of bags from the warehouse of the worker supply division, and we, at first three of us—I, A.G. Meshkov, first deputy minister of medium machine building, and Gen Antoshkin—began to fill the bags. We were soon in a sweat. We worked just the way we were: Meshkov and I in Moscow suits and street shoes and the general in his dress uniform. All without respirators and dosimeters. I soon involved in this effort Antonshchuk, manager of the trust Yuzhatomenergomontazh, his chief engineer A.I. Zayats, Yu.N. Bypiraylo, administration chief of GEM, and others. Antonshchuk ran up to me with a list of benefits which in this situation I considered comical, but I approved it on the spot. Antonshchuk and those who were about to go to work were operating according to the old pattern, not understanding that the 'dirty' zone was now everywhere, that benefits would have to be paid to everyone who lived in the city. I did not intend to distract people with explanations. There was a job to be done. But there were not enough people arriving. I asked A.I. Zayats, chief engineer of Yuzhatomenergomontazh, to go to nearby kolkhozes and ask for help...."

It is hard to imagine a scene as desperate as those three men pouring sand into the huge reactor by hand, and it soon became obvious that they were no match for the job and would need help. Naturally, it was hard to find volunteers for such a task, and Anatoliy Ivanovich Zayats explained the difficulties: "Antonshchuk and I went to the farms on the 'Druzhba' Kolkhoz. We went from farm to farm. The people were working in plots around the house. But many were out in the fields. It was spring, planting time. We began to explain that the soil was already unsuitable, that the throat of the reactor had to be plugged up, and that we needed help. It had been very hot since morning. People were in a Sunday, preholiday frame of mind. They had trouble believing us. They went on working. Then we found the kolkhoz chairman and secretary of the party organization. They went into the fields with us. We explained over and over again. Finally, people looked at us with understanding. Some 150 volunteers gathered—men and women. After that, they worked loading the bags into the helicopters without stopping. And it was all done without respirators or other safety devices. On 27 April, they supported 110 helicopter flights, on 28 April, 300 helicopter flights...."

Ultimately, that is how the people around Chernobyl filled in the belching reactor with sand. In doing so, they likely both endangered and saved their lives, for while they were exposed to more radiation than they would have been if they had not helped, they were exposed to less than they would have been if no one had done anything.

Chapter 8: The Dozens of Those Who Died

"I am thinking about the dozens of those who died, those whose names we know, and the many unborn, the lives interrupted, whose names we will never learn, since they died because of interruption of the pregnancy of women irradiated in Pripyat on 26 and 27 April. ... These were operators and firemen. The doctors continue the fight for the lives of the other serious and less serious patients. Staff members from the headquarters of USSR Minenergo have kept watch in the clinic, helping the medical personnel." - Grigoriy Medvedev

Many of the men critically injured during the explosion at Chernobyl spent their last days in one of several hospitals near the power plant, but some did survive their injuries and exposure and lived to describe what it was like for overwhelmed medical staffs to risk their own lives to save others. V.G. Smagin, whose shift at the plant followed Akimov's, recalled, "They sat the five of us down in the ambulance and took us off to the medical unit in Pripyat. They used the RUP to measure everyone's radioactivity. We washed several times. We were still radioactive. There were several therapists in the room for physicians; Lyudmila Ivanovna Prilepskaya immediately took me off to her office; her husband was also a unit shift chief, and our families were friendly. But at this point, the other lads and I began vomiting. We saw a bucket or a wastebasket, we took it and three of us at once began to vomit into that bucket. Prilepskaya asked where I had been in the unit and what the radiation fields were there? She simply could not understand that there were fields there everywhere, that it was dirty everywhere. The entire nuclear plant was an unbroken radiation field. I told her what I could between bouts of vomiting. I said that none of us knew exactly what the fields were. They were off scale at 1,000 microroentgens per second, and that was all."

Fortunately, Smagin suffered less exposure than most of his comrades, and even while still being treated himself, he was able to encourage others around him. He explained, "They put the IV needle in my vein. After about 2 hours, I began to feel vigor in my body. When the IV was finished, I stood up and began to look for a smoke. There were two others there in the ward. On one bed, a guard who was an ensign. He kept saying: 'I am going to get away from here and go home. My wife and children are worried. They do not know where I am. And I do not know what has happened to them.' 'Just lie still,' I told him. 'You have taken rems, now get your treatment...' On the other bed was a young adjuster from the Chernobyl startup and adjustment enterprise. When he learned that Volodya Shashenok had died in the morning, it seems at 0600 hours, then he began to shout why had they concealed it from him that he was dead, why hadn't they told him? He was hysterical. And he seemed to have taken fright. If Shashenok had died, that meant that he could also die. He shouted out loud: 'They are concealing everything, hiding everything...! Why didn't they tell me?!' Then he calmed down, but then he was seized with an exhausting bout of hiccupping."

The ironic thing about the hospital in Pripyat was that it was in constant danger of becoming a radioactive hot spot itself. After all, as Smagin noted, "It was 'dirty' in the medical unit. The instrument showed radioactivity. They had mobilized women from Yuzhatomenergomontazh. They were constantly washing the floors in the corridor and in the wards. The dosimetrist would come and measure everything. He kept muttering all the time: 'They wash and they wash, but it is still dirty...'"

Yuvchenko, who had held the door open for three others to attempt the impossible and inevitably fatal job of lowering the radioactive control rods, ended up in the hospital with an exposure of radiation that could easily have been lethal. During his first hours at the medical facility he was interviewed by one nurse and three KGB officers, and after he was judged to be healthy enough to travel, he was sent by bus to Moscow for special treatment. Five of those riding with him that day died shortly after they arrived in the city, and when he arrived at the facility, the attendants shaved his head and settled him in a ward. Soon, he began to develop a deep but non-productive cough, rashes on his face and lips, and serious attacks of nausea and vomiting. In time, the vomiting subsided, but by then, his skin cells had started to die off faster than his body could replace them. For a awhile, he awoke each morning to a pile of black dust that had fallen off his body the night before. He also developed deep tissue wounds on the parts of his body that had held open the door to the room housing the radioactive rods. In fact, the wounds were so bad in some places that he nearly lost one of his heavily muscled arms. Though he was able to keep it, it took seven years for the wound to heal. In the end he spent the next three years of his life in the hospital and a rehabilitation facility, but he remained upbeat enough to joke on one occasion, "The doctors told me that if you've survived this, you shouldn't worry about anything else."

Of course, not everyone was so fortunate. Lyudmilla Ignatenko lost her husband, Vasily, one of the firefighters sent to fight the blaze at the power plant. She went on to describe his last days: "At the morgue they said, 'Want to see what we'll dress him in?' I do! They dressed him up in formal wear, with his service cap. They couldn't get shoes on him because his feet had swelled up. They had to cut up the formal wear, too, because they couldn't get it on him, there wasn't a whole body to put it on. It was all — wounds. The last two days in the hospital — I'd lift his arm, and meanwhile the bone is shaking, just sort of dangling, the body has gone away from it. Pieces of his lungs, of his liver, were coming out of his mouth. He was choking on his internal organs. I'd wrap my hand in a bandage and put it in his mouth, take out all that stuff. It's impossible to talk about. It's impossible to write about. And even to live through. It was all mine."

Chapter 9: The Ash Fell on Pripyat

"Toward evening, on 9 May, at approximately 2030 hours, a part of the graphite in the reactor began burning, a void had formed under the load that had been dumped, and that whole cumbersome pile of 5,000 tons of sand, clay, and boron carbide went crashing down, hurling an immense amount of nuclear ash upward from beneath itself. The radioactivity rose sharply at the plant, in Pripyat—in the 30-km zone. The rise in radioactivity was even felt 60 km away in

Ivankov and at other places. In the darkness that had already come on, they took up the helicopter with difficulty and measured the radioactivity. The ash fell on Pripyat and surrounding fields." - Grigoriy Medvedev

As soon as the crisis in the plant had stabilized, the Russian government began sending in teams of "liquidators" to clean up the radioactive mess left behind. During the first year after the meltdown alone, more than 200,000 workers were sent into the plant, one of whom was a man named Sergei B. He explained, "My brigade was headquartered nearby the village named Oranoe. I felt that I possessed the necessary knowledge and skills to do the work required - I had my secondary (military) education as an officer-chemist. At that time, in 1986, Ph.D. scientists had 'carte blanche' - they had a power to decline the draft call (army reserve); around May-June of 1986 there was a massive call-on for mid-rank officer staff because of the high personnel rotation in early 'liquidation' campaign, and Ph.D. scientists were sort of "untouchables". But I volunteered anyway. I was 30 years old. I was a Lecturer/Scientist at the Institute of Chemical Technology, Dnepropetrovsk. I did not have a clue what was going on in until I've got there. Even after first couple of weeks it was hard to get a real picture, a grasp on the scale of operations and money tossed in the fix-up efforts. Only sometime early August I realized that this is far beyond one country problem - it is global..."

While many of these workers were members of the military, others were civilians coerced through a combination of threats and promises to work in the destroyed plant. Natalia Manzurova agreed to work on the clean-up, but she later regretted her decision: "I had no idea and never knew the true scope until much later. It was all covered in secrecy. I went there as a professional because I was told to -- but if I was asked to liquidate such an accident today, I'd never agree. ... It was like a war zone where a neutron bomb had gone off. I always felt I was in the middle of a war where the enemy was invisible. All the houses and buildings were intact with all the furniture, but there wasn't a single person left. Just deep silence everywhere. Sometimes I felt I was the only person alive on a strange planet. There are really no words to describe it."

Many of the workers were proud of the jobs they were doing, as Sergei noted, "It wasn't a feeling of the doomsday, it was an appreciation of what we are going to do, an understanding that it has to be done no matter what. Tremendous boost of the confidence. That helped to curtail the 'I do risk my life here' precautionary sense." However, optimism did not make the work any less dangerous, another fact Sergei knew all too well: "Time on the roof varied from as short as 45 sec. to as long as 3 min depending on the current radiation level and place you have to work on. Sometimes, especially after helicopter's treatment (they have used special solutions to suppress the radiation/dust by dumping tons and tons of de-activating solution very early in the morning, before we start working there), levels were not as high, so you we were able to work a bit longer. We chopped asphalt which contained pieces of highly radioactive solids sunk into molten asphalt on the explosion day (the asphalt solidified over them after the initial fire was put down...) and tossed them down on the ground, over the roof edge. Last couple of raids I primarily guided my squad/troops, simply because my cumulative dose was already too high and I was not 'allowed' to accumulate more than 1.5 Roentgen per trip... which was a travesty anyway. We had parts of General Military Protective Kit (boots, gloves, head gear...), a heavy industrial respirator, and a unique "protective piece" of two thin (about 1/8 - 1/4 in.) rectangular lead plates, about 1.5 by 2.0 ft, covering front and back. They were tied together."

Thanks to his rank and experience, Sergei was stationed at Chernobyl longer than most of the other liquidators, which meant he was exposed to more radiation than most of the other liquidators. As a result, he saw just how heavily workers were shuffled in and out: "I had to lead and to be responsible for a safe and efficient operation of troop squad ranging from 10 to 25 soldiers (army reservists). The rotation of the troops was unbelievable: there was not a single day - and I had 15 trips/days in the row during one stretch in August... - when I had more than 2-3 guys from the previous day with me. I barely remembered their names, forget faces - just because most of the time we were wearing masks/respirators, so it was really hard to recognize a person. ...I was involved in all major clean-up operations ranging from the roof of 3rd reactor (highest radiation levels) to corridors of 1+2 reactor building clean-up (lowest, probably, at the time). We also had a task to build a barb-wire fence around the whole station at some point, just to increase a security level. Different story."

As a result, those who worked cleaning up Chernobyl were both victims and heroes of the disaster, since many of them contracted the very sicknesses they worked so hard to spare others from getting. All the while, the workers were being exposed to more radiation than anyone was willing to admit. According to Sergei, "I had accumulated the sacred number - 25 Roentgens. In reality my dose was at least trice higher (according to my estimates) - during my time in the Zone, we did not have individual dosimeters whatsoever, the dose was calculated based on the 'average' working irradiation measurements, 6-8 check-points on the perimeter/mid-section of the operational field, surface, etc. Based on the 'level', the squad leader such as myself determined the average time of work, considering daily dose of 2.5 Roentgens (not higher) per person. ...there was not enough of individual dosimeters available during spring-summer of 1986 for everybody; only 'civics', engineers and scientists, had them. We, 'military', army reservists, did not. Shortage was a common word. Another reason was that it was not enough subs/rotation available, particularly of mid-rank officers, so doses accumulated by many of us during July-August-September of 1986 were artificially lowered in the paperwork."

A Soviet medal awarded to the "liquidators"

Making matters worse, the secrecy surrounding the Chernobyl disaster was so strong that the government even avoided paying many of those involved in the clean-up directly for their work. Sergei explained, "I was paid after I've got back, but strangely enough, it was a pay-off by my Institute, not by the government. Ukrainian Government picked up the tab of my pension - which wasn't that big after initial hefty paycheck after the USSR had collapsed (initial payment was about 5 times my monthly salary for those 3+ months I was in Chernobyl... this was specific extra pay for 'dangerous environment work')... it was always a very pitiful feeling to go and get my pension. After first year people quickly forgot about who we are and what we did for them... became intolerant of our (liquidator's) benefits. I have heard a lot of angry mumbling behind my back when I used a certificate - which I did quite seldom anyway...I had some health issues (heart, kidneys, etc.), which were somewhat contained not because of the government help, but because of my connections/networking - I have several friends among prominent doctors back home.... So I was more or less fortunate to get straightened out without spending time in the hospital, and then continued to work at my Institute as Associate Professor. ... I also was very careful and did not do stupid things like eating contaminated fruits and vegetables, as many of my fellow liquidators did in the Zone."

As the state broadcast and the issue over paying workers made painfully clear, the Soviet government wanted to avoid taking blame for the full extent of the disaster and the health problems that workers and citizens alike subsequently developed. One of those stricken was clean-up worker Natalia Manzurova, who later developed thyroid cancer and described the debilitating effects: "I started to feel as if I had the flu. I would get a high temperature and start to shiver. What happens during first contact with radiation is that your good flora is depleted and the bad flora starts to flourish. I suddenly wanted to sleep all the time and eat a lot. It was the organism getting all the energy out ... I knew the danger. All sorts of things happened. One colleague stepped into a rainwater pool and the soles of his feet burned off inside his boots. But I felt it was my duty to stay. I was like a firefighter. Imagine if your house was burning and the firemen came and then left because they thought it was too dangerous. They found it during a routine medical inspection after I had worked there several years. It turned out to be benign. I don't know when it started to develop. I had an operation to remove half the thyroid gland. The tumor grew back, and last year I had the other half removed. I live on (thyroid) hormones now. Right around the time of my operation, the government passed a law saying the liquidators had to work for exactly 4 1/2 years to get our pension and retire. If you left even one day early, you would not get any benefits. ... I was basically disabled at 43. I was having fits similar to epileptic fits. My blood pressure was sky high. It was hard to work for more than six months a year. The doctors didn't know what to do with me. They wanted to put me in a psychiatric ward and call me crazy. Finally they admitted it was because of the radiation."

By the time the plant was considered clean enough to end their work there, more than 600,000 men and women had thrown themselves into dealing with the fallout created in only a few minutes by the explosions. Even by that point, the countryside around Chernobyl looked nothing like it had in the happy days before the meltdown. Sergei explained, "I had a chance to go to Pripyat'. It was an eerie experience - a true ghost city. Abandoned dogs (I haven't seen cats - I think they were eventually exterminated by stronger animals...) were quite dangerous back then. I also had a chance to meet a few former station workers on the roads - they were scavenging their belongings from the city despite government's ban. This was really heart-breaking. My cousin worked on ChAES as an electrician; his younger son, my nephew, became very sick (they were staying home on that weekend... in Pripyat') and up until now he still cannot recover. At the time I had visited Pripyat', there was no people allowed to live there, there was barb wire all around, and MPs were patrolling the empty roads on BTRs; if I remember correctly, it was around mid-August, but I might be wrong. Many still did not believe that radiation is an imminent threat. I saw people fishing in contaminated river, gathering and eating potatoes, mushrooms, etc. Whoever was scared, fled the area way too fast. Who's left, were just sad and very upset with the absence of help - on any level. Locals called the accident 'the war'..."

Timm Suess' picture of Pripyat's "Red Forest," destroyed by Chernobyl's radioactive fallout, along with a radioactivity warning sign

Picture of an abandoned residence near Pripyat

The Soviet Union would not actually admit how destructive the Chernobyl accident was until radioactive fallout started making its way across Europe and spiked readings noticeably enough in Sweden for people to understand something had happened. In the wake of the disaster, Soviet investigations would be joined by international ones, but while the IAEA concluded that the accident was caused by human error and exacerbated by the lack of necessary training and experience, Soviet investigations determined the explosions were caused by design flaws.

Of course, regardless of the cause, the incredible extent of contamination made large parts of the Soviet Union uninhabitable in the years after the disaster, not to mention the toll it took on people and wildlife in the area. In many ways, the debate over the damage is ongoing, as doctors and researchers continue to debate how many have been and will be affected by ailments related to the radioactive fallout, and it's been estimated that the area around Chernobyl will be contaminated for up to 100 years.

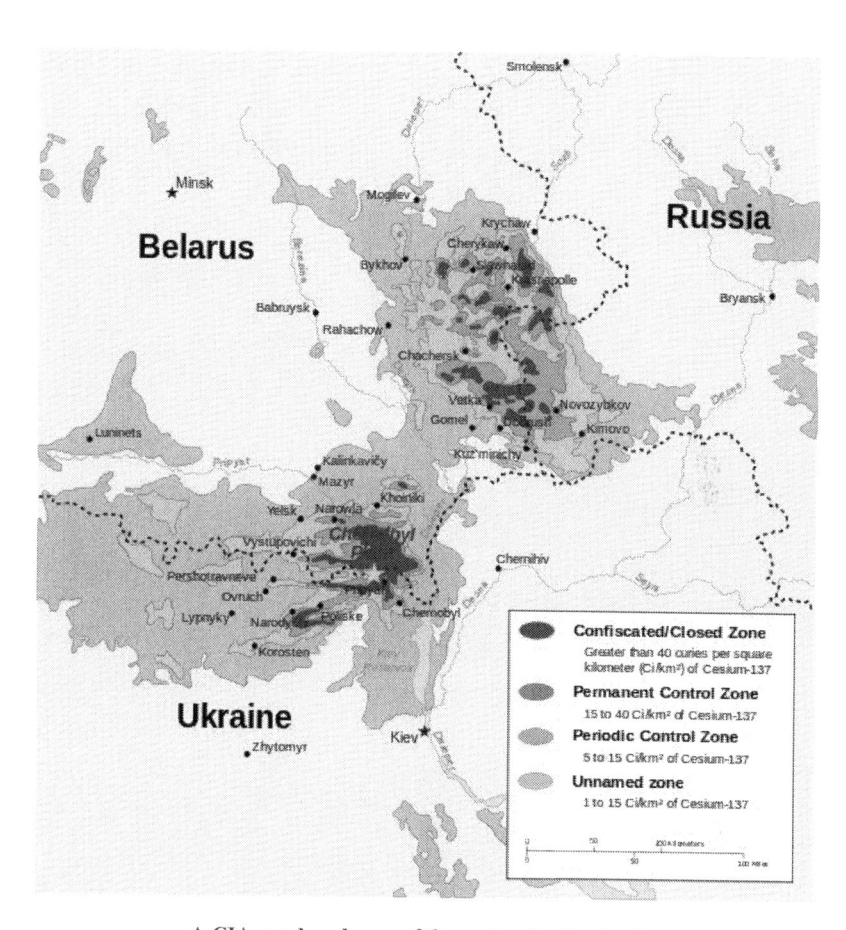

A CIA-produced map of the contamination levels

A 2003 picture of a worker monitoring the radiation level at the abandoned Chernobyl plant

Picture of the entrance to the sealed off zone around Chernobyl

Picture of abandoned buildings in Chernobyl

A picture of the "Chernobyl Nuclear Power Plant sarcophagus," designed to contain the Unit 4 reactor at Chernobyl after the accident

Tim Porter's 2013 picture of the ongoing work being done upon the New Safe Confinement, which will eventually replace the sarcophagus over Unit 4.

Bibliography

Cheney, Glenn Alan (1995). *Journey to Chernobyl: Encounters in a Radioactive Zone.* Academy Chicago.

Hoffmann, Wolfgang (2001). *Fallout From the Chernobyl Nuclear Disaster and Congenital Malformations in Europe.* Archives of Environmental Health.

Medvedev, Grigori (1989). *The Truth About Chernobyl.* VAAP. First American edition published by Basic Books in 1991.

Medvdev, Zhores A. (1990). *The Legacy of Chernobyl* (Paperback. First American edition published in 1990 ed.). W. W. Norton & Company.

Read, Piers Paul (1993). *Ablaze! The Story of the Heroes and Victims of Chernobyl.* Random House UK (paperback 1997).

Shcherbak, Yurii (1991/1989). *Chernobyl* (in Russian/English). New York: Soviet Writers/St.

Martin's Press.

Printed in Great Britain
by Amazon